WESTFIELD PUBLIC LIE
333 West Hoover Stre
Westfield, IN 46074

S0-BZW-470

Discarded by
Westfield Washington
Public Library

Read-About® Health

Fruits and Vegetables

By Susan DerKazarian

Consultants
Reading Adviser
Nanci R. Vargus, EdD
Assistant Professor of Literacy
University of Indianapolis, Indianapolis, Indiana

Subject Adviser
Janet M. Gilchrist, PhD, RD
Nutritionist

Children's Press®
A Division of Scholastic Inc.
New York   Toronto   London   Auckland   Sydney
Mexico City   New Delhi   Hong Kong
Danbury, Connecticut

Designer: Herman Adler Design
Photo Researcher: Caroline Anderson
The photo on the cover shows different sources of fruits and vegetables.

Library of Congress Cataloging-in-Publication Data

DerKazarian, Susan, 1969–
  Fruits and vegetables / by Susan DerKazarian.
    p. cm. — (Rookie read-about health)
  Includes index.
  ISBN 0-516-23673-3 (lib. bdg.)   0-516-25926-1 (pbk.)
  1. Fruit—Juvenile literature. 2. Vegetables—Juvenile literature. I. Title.
II. Series.
  TX397.D47 2005
  641.3'5—dc22   2005004776

© 2005 by Scholastic Inc.
All rights reserved. Published simultaneously in Canada.
Printed in the United States of America.

CHILDREN'S PRESS, and ROOKIE READ-ABOUT®,
and associated logos are trademarks and/or registered trademarks
of Scholastic Library Publishing. SCHOLASTIC and associated logos
are trademarks and/or registered trademarks of Scholastic Inc.

1 2 3 4 5 6 7 8 9 10 R 14 13 12 11 10 09 08 07 06 05

Eat your fruits and vegetables! Has anyone ever said that to you before?

You probably want to know why it is important to eat fruits and vegetables.

Fruits and vegetables are good for you. They have many nutrients in them.

You need nutrients to stay healthy.

The nutrients in fruits and vegetables help your heart, eyes, and skin stay healthy.

The vitamin C in grapefruit helps you fight a cold. The fiber in apples is good for your heart.

10

Apples and grapefruits are two examples of fruit. Others are oranges, peaches, watermelons, and strawberries.

These foods come from plants. Fruits usually taste sweet and have seeds.

Some examples of vegetables are carrots, potatoes, celery, and squash.

Vegetables often come from leafy plants. They usually do not taste sweet.

13

14

Most fruits grow on trees, vines, and bushes.

Vegetables usually grow in the ground.

It is important to eat fruits and vegetables every day.

17

MyPyramid.gov
STEPS TO A HEALTHIER YOU

Grain Group
Make half your grains whole

Vegetable Group
Vary your veggies

Fruit Group
Focus on fruits

Milk Group
Get your calcium-rich foods

Meat & Bean Group
Go lean with protein

Scientists came up with the Food Guidance System. It tells you how many times a day you should eat different foods to stay healthy.

Don't forget to eat at least two servings of fruits each day. You should have at least three servings of vegetables.

Be sure to eat different kinds. Choose fruits or vegetables that are different colors.

Try something new!

21

22

How can you get your two servings of fruits?

Maybe eat an apple or a banana to get one serving.

For the other, drink a glass of orange juice or snack on a handful of raisins.

Here is a way to get the vegetables you need. Throughout the day, eat a small salad, a few carrot sticks, and some mashed potatoes.

Fruits and vegetables taste good. They are also good for you.

Remember to eat them every day!

29

Words You Know

apple

carrots

celery

oranges

peaches

potatoes

squash

watermelon

31

Index

About the Author

Susan DerKazarian is senior editor at Mondo Publishing in New York City, where she helps publish books for children. In her spare time, Susan enjoys writing children's books, reading, going to the beach, and hiking.

Photo Credits

Photographs © 2005: Corbis Images: 10 bottom right (Lew Robertson), 3 (Royalty-Free); Envision Stock Photography Inc.: 13 top left, 29, 30 top right (Mark Ferri), 21 (Rita Maas), 13 top right, 31 top right (George Mattei), 13 bottom right, 31 bottom left (Steven Needham); Getty Images: 10 bottom left, 31 bottom right (Burke/Triolo Productions), 9, 30 top left (Paul Conrath/ PhotoDisc Red); Jay Mallin Photos: 25; Masterfile/G. Biss: 10 top right, 31 top left; Photo Researchers, NY: cover (Mark Burnett), 10 top left, 30 bottom right (Nigel Cattlin); PhotoEdit/Michael Newman: 13 bottom left, 22, 30 bottom left; photolibrary.com/Banana Stock: 26; Photri Inc./R. Solari: 6; PictureQuest/Ron Chapple: 14; Randy Matusow: 17; TRIP Photo Library/Rex Bamber: 5.